SALAD DRESSINGS

SALAD DRESSINGS

HAMLYN

First published in 1998
by Hamlyn
an imprint of Reed Consumer Books Limited
Michelin House, 81 Fulham Road, London SW3 6RB
and Auckland, Melbourne, and Singapore.

ISBN 0 600 59526 9

Printed in China

Special Photography: Peter Myers
Home Economist: Sunil Vijayakar
Other Photography: William Adams-Lingwood, Graham Kirk and Sandra Lane

Contents

SALAD DRESSINGS

The secret of a good salad is its dressing. Not only does a dressing add flavor and interest but it also marries its individual ingredients into a harmonious whole. A well dressed salad relies on the imagination, instinct, and individual flair of the cook as well as the way in which the ingredients are brought together. It is essential that the dressing used is suited to the ingredients — it should always enhance them rather than disguise them. For example, a piquant dressing will compliment strongly flavored meats, game, peppery watercress, and arugula, but chicken, fish, and more delicate salad leaves require lighter seasoning. Thus a good dressing brings out the flavor of the ingredients — it does not overwhelm them. It should be unobtrusive but not bland; flavorful but not overpowering.

Salad dressings are not new culinary inventions — a basic mixture of olive oil, vinegar or lemon juice, and salt has been used since ancient times in the countries bordering the Mediterranean Sea. Nowadays you can go into any deli or food market and choose from a wide range of dressings, but why buy ready-made ones when you can mix a superior one yourself in minutes, using the finest and freshest ingredients?

Types of dressings

Apart from the classic vinaigrette, there are many types of dressings, including mayonnaise, yogurt- and cream-based mixtures, and special seafood dressings, many of which are featured in this book. The most widely used dressings are as follows:

Vinaigrette

A basic vinaigrette is made with a blend of oil, vinegar, and seasonings, which may include mustard, salt, pepper, and garlic. The oil and vinegar are blended usually in the ratio of three to one. This dressing can be made in advance and stored in the refrigerator until needed.

Mayonnaise

A good mayonnaise is a creamy, shining amalgamation of egg yolks and olive oil, flavored with mustard, garlic, lemon juice, or vinegar. It is relatively easy to make and once you have mastered the technique, you can enjoy experimenting with its many variations, including aioli (a Provençal garlic mayonnaise), tartare sauce (excellent with fish), and rouille, which is often served with the great fish soups of southern France. Mayonnaise is often used to dress fish, seafood, and potato salads.

Oils

Olive oil is most commonly used, but it is not the only one. You can also try the following:

Corn oil

This is made from maize and although it is suitable for making mayonnaise, it is not ideal for vinaigrette-type salad dressings as it has quite a harsh flavor.

Herb oils

These oils are flavored with sprigs of fresh herbs, such as basil, rosemary, tarragon, or thyme. They can be savory or sweet, such as those made with elderflower.

Nut oils

Almost tasteless and odorless, peanut oil is preferred by people who dislike the strong flavor of olive oil. Consequently, it is often used in dressings. Walnut oil, with its light, nutty flavor, is more expensive. It is extracted cold from dried walnuts.

Olive oil

The oil par excellence for most salad dressings. There are many types and grades of olive oil, depending on its country of origin and extraction. Olive oil is graded according to its level of acidity. Most olive oil comes from the Mediterranean-from Spain, France, Italy, and Greece. The Spanish oils tend to be strongly flavored and an acquired taste for some, whereas the Greek oils, especially those made with Kalamata olives, are more green and fruity. It is generally acknowledged that the finest oils come from Italy and southern France. Different grades of olive oil are available, including:

Extra virgin olive oil

This oil is made from the first cold pressing of the olives and is the best oil to use for salad dressings. Delicious, full flavored and often green in color, it is the most expensive oil to buy.

Virgin olive oil

This is usually paler and more yellow in color. It is made from the second and subsequent pressings and is lighter in flavor than extra virgin oil. Use it in light salad dressings and mayonnaise. Other vegetable oils just do not have the same flavor and it is always worth investing in a good olive oil. It should be kept in a cool place but not the refrigerator as it will solidify at low temperatures. It is affected adversely by light and is better stored in cans or dark glass bottles rather than clear ones. The oil container should always be sealed or stoppered as the olive oil will turn rancid if it is kept in an open container for too long.

Sesame oil

This Chinese oil is made from sesame seeds and is sometimes used in Oriental dressings. It has a rich, nutty flavor and should be used sparingly or it will overwhelm the other ingredients. Remember that a little sesame oil goes a long way.

Truffle oil

This really is a luxurious oil for discerning gourmets. Available from some speciality stores and gourmet food sections of markets, it is a light oil perfumed with the scent of truffles.

Vinegars

Mixed together with oil, vinegar is the other essential ingredient in a classic vinaigrette. Again, there are many vinegars from which to choose.

Balsamic vinegar

Sweet, mellow, flavorful, and mild, this is the renowned pièce de rèsistance of vinegars, which is now beloved of many chefs. Made in Modena, in northern Italy, balsamic vinegar is matured in wooden casks for up to twenty years. Dark and pungent, it is often somewhat expensive but worth every cent.

Champagne vinegar

This fashionable vinegar is made with champagne but is probably not much more flavorsome than regular white wine vinegar.

Cider vinegar

Made from apple cider, this is a very healthy vinegar and less acidic than wine vinegars.

Fruit vinegars

These are very popular, the most widely used ones being raspberry and cherry vinegar. They are quite easy to make yourself at home. To make raspberry vinegar, put one pound of raspberries in a pan with 2½ cups of water and bring to a boil. Simmer, uncovered, for 20 minutes, then remove from the heat and add 4 cups of white wine vinegar and 2 cups of sugar. Stir to dissolve, then boil again, and simmer for 10 minutes. Strain into bottles when cool.

Herb vinegars

Herbs, especially rosemary and tarragon, can be used as flavorings for wine vinegars. You can make your own by putting sprigs of fresh herbs in bottles or jars and then adding warm white wine or cider vinegar. Seal and shake, then leave in a sunny place for two weeks, remembering to shake every day. Strain if wished and add fresh herbs to the vinegar.

Rice vinegar

This is a light, mildly flavored Japanese vinegar, which compliments fish salads and Oriental food. Naturally sweet, it is available in the Oriental sections of many gourmet stores and markets.

Sherry vinegar

With a rich, sweet, and subtle flavor, this aged vinegar is made with Spanish sherry and is often used in nouvelle cuisine-type salads.

Wine vinegars

These are made from any wine untreated with preservatives and may be red or white. The most commonly used is white wine vinegar, especially in vinaigrettes, but red wine vinegar is excellent added to warm dressings and more robust salads, such as those made with cold meats or root vegetables.

Successful salad tips

- When dressing a salad, timing makes all the difference between success and failure. Mixing salad leaves with a dressing must always be done at the very last minute–immediately before serving. If it is dressed too early, the leaves will wilt and rapidly become soggy and unappetizing, or, as the French are known to say, "fatigué" (tired).

- Be sure to wash all leaves and vegetables thoroughly to remove any dirt and traces of chemical sprays before assembling the salad. Dry very thoroughly by spinning or patting dry with paper towels, or the dressing will not cling to the ingredients, and the salad will be soggy and watery.

- Always prepare the salad and dressing separately and then toss together lightly before serving or serve the dressing separately in a jug. Do not add oil, vinegar, or other dressing ingredients to the salad without blending them well first.

- If you are a garlic fanatic, you can add a subtle garlic flavor to a salad by rubbing a cut garlic clove around the inside of the salad bowl before adding the salad ingredients and dressing.

Storage and freshness

Most salad dressings can be made in advance and stored in a sealed container in the refrigerator until required. Mayonnaise can also be kept in the refrigerator, preferably in a screw-top jar, for up to five days. Once dressed, most salads, especially leaf ones, are at their best eaten immediately. However, more robust salads, such as those made with potatoes and meat, can be dressed with a vinaigrette mixture and stored for up to twelve hours in the refrigerator. Salads dressed with mayonnaise have a tendency to deteriorate quickly and should really be consumed within a few hours of mixing.

Salad bowl and servers

The ideal material for salad bowls is wood, preferably a deep, straight-sided bowl to make mixing the ingredients and dressing easier. Wooden bowls should never be washed by immersing in warm, soapy water. Instead, they should be wiped with paper towels after use. Glass, ceramic, or plastic salad bowls are fine, but avoid metal bowls (with the exception of stainless steel) as the acid in the salad dressing can react with the metal.

The classic vinaigrette

There is an old French saying that it takes four men to make a good vinaigrette: a spendthrift for the oil, a miser for the vinegar, a wise man for the salt, and a madman for the pepper. The standard proportions for a vinaigrette are three parts oil to one part vinegar, but this can vary according to individual taste and the type of oil and vinegar used. As listed earlier, olive, peanut, walnut, or flavored oils are all suitable, and the variety

you choose will depend on the ingredients in the salad. For example, some olive oils are so strongly flavored that they can overwhelm a delicate salad, whereas a more subtle nut oil will enhance the salad. You can choose from balsamic, cider, fruit, herb, sherry, or wine vinegars, or, alternatively, you can use freshly squeezed lemon juice instead, as practiced in Greece and the Middle East. Salt and pepper are essential, and most French chefs will also add a teaspoon of a good Dijon mustard, sometimes with a pinch of sugar, to emulsify the dressing. To make the vinaigrette, simply whisk the vinegar and seasonings (see below) together until smooth, then whisk in the oil, a little at a time, until the mixture thickens. If the dressing separates on standing, simply whisk it again before dressing the salad.

Flavorings for vinaigrettes
There are many flavorings that you can add to a regular vinaigrette. Experiment with some of the following:

- Minced garlic
- Seeded, finely chopped chilies
- Finely chopped onion or shallot
- Finely chopped or torn fresh herbs
- Finely grated Parmesan cheese
- Lemon and orange juice and finely grated zest
- Soy sauce to Oriental dressings
- Grated fresh root ginger and spices
- Dijon mustard
- Mashed avocado
- Chopped capers and pitted olives
- Crumbled, grilled crispy bacon bits
- Chopped anchovy fillets
- Chopped toasted nuts, e.g. almonds, cashews, peanuts or walnuts

- Mashed or chopped hard-boiled egg
- Diced cheese, e.g. feta, Swiss, or blue cheese
- Sautèed sliced exotic mushrooms

Croûtons
These are small, crisp, golden brown cubes of baked, fried, or toasted bread, often flavored with garlic or herbs. Essential for a Caesar salad, croûtons can also be scattered over salad leaves just before mixing with the dressing and serving. To make quick croûtons, just toss small cubes of bread in some olive oil, add some chopped herbs or minced garlic if wished, and place on a cookie sheet. Bake in a preheated hot oven at 400°F for 6–8 minutes, until crisp and golden.

Warm salad dressings
These are now very much in vogue, especially with the fashion for wilted salad leaves-usually spinach and arugula. You can make a warm dressing by sautéing some chopped onion, garlic, or mushrooms in olive oil in a skillet and then deglazing the skillet with balsamic or wine vinegar. Season and pour the warm dressing over the salad. Serve immediately.

CLASSIC VINAIGRETTE

Serve this classic dressing with a classic tomato, cucumber and onion salad
and garnish with chopped parsley.

¾ cup olive oil
4 tablespoons white wine vinegar, cider vinegar or tarragon vinegar
1 teaspoon clear honey
2 tablespoons chopped mixed herbs eg mint, parsley, chives, thyme
1 garlic clove, minced
salt and pepper

Beat the oil with the chosen vinegar, honey, herbs, garlic, and salt and pepper to taste until well blended. Alternatively, place all the ingredients in a screw-top jar and shake vigorously to combine well before using.

Makes 1 cup

VARIATION
LEMON AND LIME VINAIGRETTE

¾ cup olive oil
2 tablespoons lemon juice
2 tablespoons lime juice
1 teaspoon clear honey
1 garlic clove, crushed
2 tablespoons, chopped mixed herbs, e.g. mint, parsley, chives, thyme
salt and pepper

Beat the oil with the lemon and lime juices, honey, garlic, herbs, and salt and pepper to taste until well blended. Alternatively, place all the ingredients in a screw-top jar, and shake vigorously to combine well before using.

Makes 1 cup

VERMOUTH DRESSING

The perfect dressing for a Cobb Salad.

½ cup olive oil
4 tablespoons white wine vinegar
2 tablespoons dry white vermouth
pinch of sugar
2 tablespoons chopped parsley
1 tablespoon chopped chives
salt and freshly ground black pepper

Beat the oil with the vinegar, vermouth, sugar, chopped herbs, and salt and pepper to taste until well blended. Alternatively, place all the ingredients in a screw-top jar and shake vigorously to combine well before using.

Makes about 1 cup

CRANBERRY VINAIGRETTE

This is a perfect dressing to use on leftover turkey. Slice the turkey into bite-size pieces and serve with quartered leaves of Belgian endive (chicory), garnished with orange slices.

4 tablespoons hazelnut oil
juice of 1 orange
1 tablespoon raspberry vinegar
or red wine vinegar
1 tablespoon cranberry sauce or jelly
⅓ cup coarsely chopped hazelnuts
salt and pepper

1 Put all the ingredients in a bowl with salt and pepper to taste and beat well to combine. Alternatively, place all the ingredients in a screw-top jar, and shake vigorously to combine well before using.
2 Beat the dressing again before serving.

Makes about 1 cup
Preparation time: 5 minutes

MIDSUMMER SALAD

This refreshing salad is delicious with a selection of cheeses or ham.

I small ripe melon
I cup strawberries, thinly sliced
I x 3-inch piece cucumber, thinly sliced
I small crisp lettuce, shredded
4 tablespoons French dressing (see below)
2 tablespoons chopped fresh mint or lemon balm
2 tablespoons slivered almonds, to garnish

French dressing:
I cup olive oil
5 tablespoons white wine vinegar
½ teaspoon French mustard
I garlic clove, minced
I teaspoon clear honey
small strip of lemon rind
few sprigs of fresh herbs
salt and pepper

1 First make the dressing. Beat together the oil, vinegar, mustard, garlic, honey, lemon rind, herbs, and salt and pepper to taste until well blended. Alternatively, place all the ingredients in a screw-top jar and shake vigorously to combine well before using.

2 Cut the melon into quarters, then remove the seeds and rind. Cut the flesh into cubes, about ½ inch square, or scoop into balls.

3 To serve, place the shredded lettuce on a large serving dish or 4 individual plates. Arrange the pieces of melon, strawberry, and cucumber on top of the lettuce.

3 Mix the French dressing with the chopped mint or lemon balm and pour it over the salad just before serving. Sprinkle with the almonds, to garnish.

Serves 4

VARIATION

Use small ogen melons, allowing half a melon per person. Arrange the salad in the scooped-out melon halves rather than on plates. Substitute sliced banana or kiwi fruit for some or all of the strawberries.

HONEY DRESSING

Dress a salad of watercress and chopped spinach leaves and sliced oranges with this tangy dressing.

4 tablespoons lemon juice
2 tablespoons clear honey
3 tablespoons olive oil
salt and pepper

Beat together the lemon juice, honey, olive oil, and salt and pepper to taste until well blended. Alternatively, place all the ingredients in a screw-top jar and shake vigorously to combine well before using.

Makes ¹/₂ cup

MINT DRESSING

This light and refreshing dressing would taste delicious with a cold potato salad or tossed lightly over a salad of chopped apples and herring.

6 tablespoons olive oil
2 tablespoons lemon juice
2–3 tablespoons chopped mint
pinch of sugar
salt and pepper

1 Beat the oil with the lemon juice, mint, sugar, and salt and pepper to taste until well blended. Alternatively, place all the ingredients in a screw-top jar and shake vigorously to combine well before serving.
2 Set aside for at least 15 minutes to allow the flavors to develop, then beat or shake again before using.

Makes about ¹/₂ cup

RASPBERRY DRESSING

The use of two oils makes this dressing all the more interesting. It is delicious with green salads
made with mild vegetables, such as zucchini.

3 tablespoons corn oil
2 tablespoons sesame oil
3 tablespoons raspberry vinegar
salt and pepper

Beat the oils with the vinegar and salt and pepper to taste until well blended. Alternatively, place all the ingredients in a screw-top jar or bottle and shake vigorously to combine well before using.

Makes ½ cup

VARIATION

You could also make this fruity salad dressing with strawberry vinegar or, should you be
so fortunate, champagne vinegar. For a minted flavor, add ½ to 1 tablespoon of finely chopped
mint to the ingredients before blending.

PORT DRESSING

This is the perfect festive season dressing for Christmas and Thanksgiving. Use it on crisp lettuce or melon salads.
A little chopped tarragon can be added just before serving to introduce a subtle flavor.

6 tablespoons corn oil
3 tablespoons red wine vinegar
⅔ cup port wine
1 teaspoon chopped tarragon (optional)
salt and pepper

1 Beat the oil with the vinegar, port wine, and salt and pepper to taste until well blended. Alternatively, place all the ingredients in a screw-top jar or bottle and shake vigorously to blend.
2 Add the tarragon, if used, just before serving, mixing or shaking well to combine.

Makes about 1 cup

BELGIAN ENDIVE AND FRUIT SALAD

5 heads of Belgian endive (chicory)
2 celery hearts, thinly sliced into rings
4 oranges, peeled and sectioned
½ pound seedless white grapes
½ pound black grapes, halved and seeded
1½ cups thinly sliced mushrooms (optional)
2 bunches watercress (optional)

Citrus spring dressing:
9 tablespoons olive oil
3 tablespoons orange juice
1 tablespoon lemon juice
1 teaspoon sugar
2 green onions, thinly sliced
salt and freshly ground black pepper

1 Thinly slice the Belgian endive heads into rings, reserving 10-12 leaves, to garnish. Toss together the sliced Belgian endive, celery, oranges, grapes, and mushrooms, if using in a bowl. Separate the watercress, if using, into sprigs and set aside.

2 Beat together all the ingredients for the dressing, with salt and pepper to taste until well blended. Alternatively, place all the ingredients in a screw-top jar and shake vigorously to combine well before using.

3 Pour the dressing over the salad about 1 hour before serving, and toss to mix well. Add the watercress just before serving and garnish with the reserved Belgian endive leaves.

Serves 4
Preparation time: 15 minutes, plus standing

SOY SAUCE DRESSING

¾ cup corn oil
4 tablespoons soy sauce
2 tablespoons lemon juice
I garlic clove, minced
salt and pepper

Beat together the corn oil, soy sauce, lemon juice, garlic, and salt and pepper to taste. Alternatively, place all the ingredients in a screw-top jar and shake vigorously to combine well before using.

Makes 1¼ cups

VARIATION

Transform this dressing into a hot chili dressing, by adding 1 seeded and finely chopped green chili and a few drops of chili oil to the recipe.

GINGER DRESSING

I x I-inch piece fresh ginger root, peeled and finely chopped
¾ cup corn oil
4 tablespoons soy sauce
2 tablespoons lemon juice
I garlic clove, minced
salt and pepper

Beat together the ginger, corn oil, soy sauce, lemon juice, garlic and salt and pepper to taste. Alternatively, place all the ingredients in a screw-top jar and shake vigorously to combine well before using.

Makes 1¼ cups

GINGER AND LIME DRESSING

This dressing has a fresh oriental flavor which complements fish, shellfish, duck, and chicken as well as many leafy salads and lightly cooked vegetables. You can prepare it in advance but should add the cilantro just before serving.

2 tablespoons grated fresh ginger root
I garlic clove, minced
2 limes
I tablespoon clear honey
5 tablespoons peanut oil
2 tablespoons chopped cilantro
salt and pepper

I Combine the ginger and garlic in a bowl. Grate the limes finely and add the zest to the bowl along with the honey. Stir in salt and pepper to taste.

2 Squeeze the juice from both limes into the bowl and beat well. Pour in the oil, beating the dressing until well mixed. Just before using, stir in the chopped cilantro.

3 Alternatively, place all the ingredients in a screw-top jar and shake vigorously to combine well before using.

4 Stir the chopped cilantro into the dressing just before serving.

Makes about 1¼ cups

RED CABBAGE, APPLE, AND CHEESE SALAD WITH SWEET MUSTARD DRESSING

½ cup pecans or walnuts, coarsely chopped
I small red cabbage, shredded
I red or white onion, thinly sliced
6 ounces fresh dates, pitted
and coarsely chopped
I large red apple, cubed
5 ounces Monterey Jack or Swiss cheese,
crumbled or cubed
salt and pepper

Sweet mustard dressing:
3 tablespoons olive oil
2 tablespoons whole-grain mustard
I tablespoon clear honey
I teaspoon white wine vinegar
or lemon juice
salt and pepper

1 Place the pecans or walnuts on a cookie sheet and toast under a preheated hot broiler for 2–3 minutes, until browned. Set aside.

2 Beat together all the ingredients for the dressing in a small bowl and beat until thoroughly blended. Alternatively, place all the ingredients in a screw-top jar and shake vigorously to combine well before using.

3 Place the cabbage in a large salad bowl with the onion, dates, and apple. Season with salt and pepper to taste and toss lightly.

4 Add the cheese to the salad and sprinkle over the reserved nuts. Pour the dressing over the salad and serve immediately.

Serves 4–6
Preparation time: 15 minutes
Cooking time: 2–3 minutes

PESTO DRESSING

The vibrant color and sensational taste of this dressing make it a treat for both the eye and the tastebuds—try this mixed with a chicken and bell pepper salad.

I ounce basil leaves
3 tablespoons grated Parmesan cheese
I tablespoon pine nuts
4 tablespoons white wine vinegar
I garlic clove, minced
½ cup extra virgin olive oil
freshly ground black pepper

I Combine the basil leaves, Parmesan, pine nuts, vinegar, and garlic in a blender or food processor. Season with black pepper to taste. Process for a few seconds.

2 With the blender or food processor running, add the olive oil through the feeder tube in a thin, steady stream, until the mixture becomes thick and smooth. Pour into a bowl or jug and use as required.

Makes about I cup
Preparation time: 5 minutes

VARIATION
RED PESTO DRESSING

Add ¼ cup drained and sliced sun-dried tomatoes in oil to the above ingredients and blend them to a rough paste. You could also substitute half the oil from the jar for half the olive oil for an even stronger flavor.

GREEN SALAD WITH MAPLE AND CHIVE DRESSING

mixed salad leaves
chive flowers, to garnish (optional)

Maple and chive dressing:
5 tablespoons extra virgin olive oil
or nut oil
1 tablespoon raspberry or
red wine vinegar
2 tablespoons chopped chives
1 teaspoon maple syrup
salt and pepper

1 Beat together the oil, vinegar, chives, maple syrup, and salt and pepper to taste. Alternatively, place all the ingredients in a screw-top jar and shake vigorously to combine well before using. Chill for 30 minutes.

2 Put the salad leaves in a bowl, beat or shake the dressing again, and pour it over the salad. Toss well and serve garnished with chive flowers, if using.

Serves 4–6
Preparation time: 5 minutes, plus chilling

WALNUT DRESSING

Nut dressings, such as this, add interest to pasta or rice salads and are also excellent with mixed salads.

3 tablespoons balsamic vinegar or
sherry vinegar
1 teaspoon soft brown sugar
1 teaspoon Dijon mustard
salt and freshly ground black pepper
½ cup walnut oil
1 tablespoon finely chopped walnuts
1 tablespoon chopped parsley,
sage, thyme, or basil

1 Combine the vinegar, sugar, and mustard in a small bowl. Add salt and pepper to taste. Stir to mix, then gradually beat in the walnut oil, a little at a time.

2 Stir the chopped walnuts and herbs into the dressing and add a little more salt and pepper, if necessary.

Makes about ⅔ cup
Preparation time: 10 minutes

MIXED TOMATO SALAD WITH CILANTRO DRESSING

2 pounds red and yellow cherry tomatoes, sliced or quartered
2 teaspoons grated lime zest
½ small red onion, thinly sliced
I tablespoon sesame seeds, toasted

Cilantro Dressing:
2 tablespoons chopped cilantro
I tablespoon lime juice
I garlic clove, minced
½ teaspoon clear honey
pinch of cayenne pepper
4 tablespoons extra virgin olive oil
salt and pepper

1 Make the dressing. Beat together the cilantro, lime juice, garlic, honey, cayenne pepper, season with salt and pepper, and then beat in the oil.

2 Arrange the tomatoes in a large serving bowl and scatter over the lime zest, red onion, and toasted sesame seeds.

3 Beat the dressing ingredients again and pour over the salad. Cover the salad and set aside for 30 minutes to allow the flavors to develop before serving.

Serves 4
Preparation time: 5 minutes, plus marinating

BASIC MAYONNAISE

To store the mayonnaise, cover and chill in the refrigerator. Fresh mayonnaise will keep for about three days. Beat well before using.

2 egg yolks or I egg
I tablespoon white wine vinegar
or lemon juice
$\frac{1}{2}$ teaspoon salt
pinch of freshly ground white pepper
$\frac{1}{2}$ teaspoon dry mustard powder
1$\frac{1}{4}$ cups olive oil (at room temperature)

1 Put the egg yolks (or whole egg) in a bowl and beat with a hand whisk, electric blender, or a food processor on medium speed until smooth, pale, and creamy. Add the vinegar or lemon juice, salt, pepper, and mustard powder, beating until well blended.
2 Add the olive oil, drop by drop to begin with, beating constantly. When the mixture starts to thicken and emulsify, add the oil in a thin, steady stream, beating steadily to incorporate. Gradually increase the flow of the oil as the dressing thickens and becomes very creamy. Beat until the mixture is thick and does not fall off the whisk when raised above the bowl. If the mayonnaise becomes too thick, then thin it with a little extra white wine vinegar or lemon juice.

Makes 1$\frac{1}{4}$ cups
Preparation time: 15 minutes

VARIATION
TOMATO MAYONNAISE

Skin, seed, and chop 2 tomatoes and place them in a blender or food processor with 1 crushed garlic clove, $\frac{1}{2}$ teaspoon brown sugar, and 2 teaspoons tomato paste. Blend on maximum speed for 30 seconds, then stir into the mayonnaise.

Makes about 1$\frac{1}{4}$ cups
Preparation time: 15 minutes

CURRY MAYONNAISE

2 egg yolks or I egg
I tablespoon lemon juice
$\frac{1}{2}$ teaspoon salt
pinch of freshly ground white pepper
$\frac{1}{2}$ teaspoon dry mustard powder
I $\frac{1}{4}$ cups olive oil (at room temperature)
2 tablespoons chopped mixed herbs,
e.g. parsley, chives, tarragon, chervil,
rosemary, and thyme
1–2 teaspoons curry powder
I teaspoon mango chutney

I Make the mayonnaise in the usual way, (see page 28) by blending the egg and lemon juice, seasoning, and mustard powder, then adding the oil, drop by drop at first, and later in a thin stream. Add the herbs, curry powder, and mango chutney. Stir well to blend.

Makes I $\frac{1}{4}$ cups
Preparation time: 15 minutes

PARMESAN MAYONNAISE

5 tablespoons mayonnaise (see page 28)
4–5 tablespoons water
1–2 garlic cloves
3 tablespoons finely grated
Parmesan cheese
coarse sea salt
freshly ground black pepper

Put the mayonnaise in a small bowl and stir in enough of the water to make a thin, pourable sauce. Pound the garlic to a paste with a little coarse sea salt. Add this paste to the mayonnaise along with the grated Parmesan and stir well. Thin the mayonnaise mixture with a little more water, if necessary, so that the sauce remains pourable. Add black pepper to taste.

Makes $\frac{2}{3}$ cup
Preparation time: 5 minutes

CRAB LOUIS

Many versions of the Louis dressing can be found, although they are all based on a rich, piquant, mayonnaise mixture. Other types of seafood go well with the dressing, such as lobster and shrimp, and it is also excellent with a mixed seafood salad.

1 large round iceberg lettuce, shredded
1 small savoy cabbage, finely shredded
1 pound crab meat
4 tomatoes, cut into wedges
2 eggs, hard-boiled, peeled, and cut into wedges
3 green onions, shredded, to garnish

Piquant herb dressing:
1 cup mayonnaise (see page 28)
5 tablespoons tomato-based chili sauce
¼ cup finely chopped green bell pepper
3 tablespoons green onions, sliced
1 tablespoon chopped parsley
1–2 teaspoons tomato paste
1 teaspoon Worcestershire sauce
½ cup heavy cream, whipped
salt and freshly ground black pepper

1 In a bowl stir together the mayonnaise, chili sauce, bell pepper, green onions, parsley, tomato paste, Worcestershire sauce, and salt and pepper to taste. When well mixed, fold in the whipped heavy cream. Cover and refrigerate at least 1 hour.

2 When ready to serve, line a serving platter with the shredded lettuce and cabbage and pile the crab meat on top. Arrange the tomato and egg wedges around the crab meat. Spoon the dressing over the crab meat and garnish with the shredded green onion.

Serves: 4–6
Preparation time: 20 minutes, plus chilling

SPICED ORANGE MAYONNAISE

A warm, subtle, yet fresh-tasting mayonnaise dressing which is perfect to serve with any duck, game, or rich meat salads, especially those made with citrus fruits.

8 tablespoons mayonnaise (see page 28)
finely grated zest of I orange
4 teaspoons tomato paste
2 teaspoons mild curry powder
I teaspoon mustard
2 tablespoons light cream
salt and pepper

Mix the mayonnaise with the orange zest, tomato paste, curry powder, mustard, and cream, blending well. Season with salt and pepper to taste. Cover and let stand for at least 15 minutes to allow the flavors to develop.

Makes 1¼ cups
Preparation time: 5 minutes, plus standing

SAFFRON MAYONNAISE

pinch of saffron threads
I tablespoon boiling water
2 egg yolks
I tablespoon lemon juice
⅔ cups olive oil
salt and pepper

Place the saffron threads in a small bowl. Pour the boiling water over the saffron and leave to infuse for 10 minutes. Combine the egg yolks and lemon juice in a separate bowl. Add the saffron and its soaking liquid to the egg and lemon juice mixture and beat until slightly thickened. Continue to beat briskly, gradually adding the oil in a thin stream until the mixture forms a thick, creamy mayonnaise. Season with salt and pepper to taste.

Makes ¾ cup
Preparation time: 15 minutes, plus infusing

BASIL MAYONNAISE

3 tablespoons mayonnaise (see page 28)
¹/₂ ounce basil leaves, finely chopped
I small garlic clove, minced
¹/₂ teaspoon lemon juice
I tablespoon extra virgin olive oil
I tablespoon boiling water
salt and pepper

Put the mayonnaise in a bowl, and beat in the basil, garlic, lemon juice, oil, boiling water, and salt and pepper to taste.

Makes ¹/₄ cup
Preparation time: 5 minutes

AÏOLI

Aïoli is a Provençal dish. It should be very thick and smooth, with a powerful garlic flavor. Any combination of salad vegetables can be served as crudités to dip into the aïoli—sliced bell peppers, radishes, sticks of cucumber, zucchini batons, and pieces of fennel are particularly good.

2 egg yolks
6 garlic cloves, minced
¹/₂ teaspoon salt
I ¹/₄ cups olive oil
I–2 teaspoons lemon juice

1 To make the aïoli, beat the egg yolks with the garlic and salt until the mixture thickens. Add the oil, drop by drop, beating constantly. As it thickens, add 1 teaspoon lemon juice, and then add the oil in a steady stream, beating vigorously. Add the remaining lemon juice to taste and mix thoroughly.
2 Spoon the aïoli into a small bowl, place on a large plate, and surround with a selection of prepared vegetables.

Makes I ¹/₃ cups
Preparation time: 15 minutes

CAESAR SALAD

I romaine lettuce
I x 2-ounce can anchovy fillets in olive oil, drained
I small white bread loaf
¾ stick butter, melted
3 tablespoons freshly grated Parmesan cheese shavings, to garnish

Caesar dressing:
5 tablespoons mayonnaise (see page 28)
4–5 tablespoons water
I–2 garlic cloves
3 tablespoons finely grated Parmesan cheese
coarse sea salt
freshly ground black pepper

1 Start by making the dressing. Put the mayonnaise in a small bowl and stir in enough of the water to make a thin, pourable sauce. Pound the garlic to a paste with a little coarse sea salt. Add to the mayonnaise along with the Parmesan and stir well. Thin it with a little more water, if necessary, so that the sauce remains pourable. Add pepper to taste and set aside.

2 Tear the lettuce leaves into large pieces and place in a large salad bowl. Chop the anchovies into small pieces and scatter over the lettuce.

3 To make the croûtons, cut the bread into 1¼-inch thick slices. Cut off the crusts and discard. Brush the slices of bread with the melted butter and cut them into 1-inch cubes. Brush a large cookie sheet with a little of the melted butter. Arrange the bread cubes on it in a single layer, brushing the sides with any remaining butter.

4 Bake in a preheated oven at 400°F for about 12 minutes, or until the croûtons are crisp and a deep golden color. Watch the croûtons carefully after 8 minutes, as they tend to color quickly towards the end of the cooking time.

5 To serve, tip the hot croûtons into the salad and quickly drizzle the dressing over the top. Scatter the Parmesan cheese shavings over the salad and serve immediately.

Serves 4–6
Preparation time: 20 minutes
Cooking time: 12 minutes
Oven temperature: 400°F

THOUSAND ISLAND DRESSING

You can transform this mixture into a Marie Rose dressing for serving with shellfish salads by omitting the chopped parsley, bell peppers, celery, and olives.

½ **quantity mayonnaise (see page 28)**
½ **teaspoon paprika**
1 **teaspoon minced onion**
pinch of garlic salt
½ **teaspoon tomato paste**
2 **teaspoons chopped parsley**
3 **tablespoons finely chopped red bell pepper**
3 **tablespoons finely chopped green bell pepper**
2 **tablespoons finely chopped celery**
2 **green olives or 1 small gherkin, finely chopped**

Mix the mayonnaise with the paprika, onion, garlic salt, and tomato paste in a bowl. Add the parsley, bell peppers, celery, and olives or gherkin, and mix well to blend. Set aside for at least 15 minutes to allow the flavors to develop before using.

Makes 1½ cups
Preparation time: 10 minutes, plus standing

HORSERADISH AND SOUR CREAM DRESSING

This is a simple dressing but it is really delicious and very versatile. Serve it with winter vegetables, roast meat, and smoked fish. Alternatively, add chopped fresh herbs, chopped toasted nuts, minced garlic or onion, capers or olives.

1¼ cups sour cream
4 teaspoons creamed horseradish
salt and pepper

Stir the sour cream and creamed horseradish together in a bowl. Add salt and pepper to taste.

Makes 1⅓ cups
Preparation time: 1 minute

SOUR CREAM AND ORANGE DRESSING

This is a delicious creamy dressing to serve with a green salad or even to top a fruit salad.

1 cup sour cream
grated zest and juice of 1 orange
2 tablespoons lemon juice
1 teaspoon sugar
salt and pepper

Mix the sour cream with the orange zest and juice, lemon juice, and sugar. Season to taste with salt and pepper. Chill lightly, then stir well before serving.

Makes 1 cup
Preparation time: 5 minutes, plus chilling

ENGLISH GARDEN SALAD

Cauliflower, peas, and crisp rosy radishes with a creamy mint dressing—this salad is evocative of an English vegetable garden.

1 small cauliflower, broken into florets
1½ cups shelled fresh peas
1 bunch radishes, trimmed
4 green onions, chopped
2 tablespoons chopped parsley
salt and pepper
sprigs of mint and chopped flat-leaf parsley, to garnish

Mint dressing:
6 tablespoons mayonnaise (see page 28)
3 tablespoons plain yogurt
3 tablespoons water
½ garlic clove, minced (optional)
1–2 tablespoons finely chopped fresh mint
salt and pepper

1 Bring a saucepan of water to the boil and add the cauliflower florets. When the water returns to the boil, cook the florets for about 3 minutes, until just tender. Drain and refresh under cold running water, then drain thoroughly and set aside to cool.

2 Add the peas to a saucepan of boiling water. Cook for 4 minutes, then drain, refresh, and cool as for the cauliflower.

3 Combine the cauliflower, peas, radishes, and green onions in a serving bowl. Add the parsley, with salt and pepper to taste.

4 To make the dressing, stir all the ingredients together in a small bowl. Adjust the seasoning to taste. Serve the dressing on the side or drizzle over the salad and toss lightly before serving. Garnish with sprigs of mint and chopped flat-leaf parsley.

Serves: 4-6
Preparation time: 25 minutes
Cooking time: 10 minutes

TANGY CHEESE DRESSING

½ cup dolcelatte cheese (or other creamy blue cheese), softened
½ cup ricotta cheese, softened
6 tablespoons extra virgin olive oil
I tablespoon white wine vinegar
I tablespoon boiling water
salt and pepper

Blend the two cheeses together and gradually beat in the oil, vinegar, boiling water, salt and pepper to taste until a smooth, thick dressing is formed.

Makes ½ cup
Preparation time: 10 minutes

ROQUEFORT AND CHIVE DRESSING

Roquefort is a distinctive blue cheese with a rich, strong, and salty flavor.
It will probably make this salad dressing sufficiently salty for most palates, so do not add any extra salt until you have thoroughly incorporated the cheese and tasted the results. Serve with crisp green salads and potato salads. If you cannot get Roquefort, substitute another blue cheese.

¾ cup olive oil
4 tablespoons sherry vinegar or white wine vinegar
¼ cup Roquefort cheese, crumbled
2 tablespoons chopped chives
salt and pepper

1 Beat the oil with the vinegar until well blended. Place the cheese in a bowl and mash until creamy. Gradually add the oil and vinegar mixture, beating well to make a smooth creamy dressing. Fold in the chopped chives.
2 Taste the dressing and add salt and pepper, if necessary. Cover and chill until required.

Makes I cup
Preparation time: 10 minutes, plus chilling

CHEESY LEMON DRESSING

Use this deliciously smooth and creamy dressing as an alternative to mayonnaise—it is especially good with fish salads.

²/₃ **cup full-fat soft cheese**
4 tablespoons corn oil
2 tablespoons lemon juice
1 teaspoon grated lemon zest
¹/₂ teaspoon mild mustard
salt and pepper

Beat the cheese until softened, then gradually add the oil, lemon juice, and lemon zest, and mix until smooth and creamy. Season with the mustard and salt and pepper to taste. Serve lightly chilled.

Makes ²/₃ cup
Preparation time: 10 minutes, plus chilling

APHRODITE DRESSING

Serve this heavenly dressing over a tomato and onion salad, garnished with shredded fennel.

¹/₂ **cup crumbled feta cheese**
2 teaspoons chopped fresh oregano
salt and pepper
6–8 tablespoons olive oil

Place the feta cheese, oregano, and salt and pepper to taste in a bowl and mix gently. Pour over the olive oil and combine well before serving.

Makes: ²/₃ cup
Preparation time: 5 minutes

GREEK SALAD WITH TAHINI DRESSING

This salad goes well served with cold roast meats and pitta bread.

½ large cucumber
¾ pound tomatoes, cut into thin wedges
1 small green bell pepper, quartered,
seeded, and sliced
1 small onion, thinly sliced
8 small black olives, pitted and cut in half
½ cup feta cheese

Tahini dressing:
2 tablespoons tahini paste
4 tablespoons plain yogurt
1–2 tablespoons water
2 tablespoons chopped fresh parsley
1 small garlic clove, minced
salt and freshly ground black pepper

1 Cut the cucumber into ¼ inch-slices, then cut these across into ¼-inch batons, and place in a salad bowl. Add the tomatoes, green bell pepper, onion, and olives.

2 For the dressing, spoon the tahini paste into a small bowl. Slowly beat in the yogurt and thin down with the water as necessary. Stir in the parsley, garlic, and salt and pepper to taste. Pour the dressing over the salad and toss gently. Cut the feta cheese into cubes and sprinkle over the top.

Serves: 4-6
Preparation time: 15 minutes

NORMANDY DRESSING

This simple but sumptuous creamy dressing is splendid sprinkled over light, crisp, spring and summer salads that are made with a selection of young leafy vegetables.

2 tablespoons lemon juice
4 tablespoons heavy cream
$\frac{1}{2}$ teaspoon finely grated lemon zest
I tablespoon chopped chives
salt and freshly ground black pepper

Beat together the lemon juice, cream, lemon zest, chives, salt and pepper to taste in a bowl until well blended and creamy. Cover and chill in the refrigerator until required.

Makes about $\frac{1}{2}$ cup
Preparation time: 5 minutes, plus chilling

CREAMY CAPER DRESSING

This is a recipe for a rich, creamy, and piquant caper dressing that is ideal to serve with lamb or fish salads.

2 tablespoons olive oil
I $\frac{1}{2}$ teaspoons white wine vinegar
3 hard-boiled egg yolks
2 teaspoons Dijon mustard
$\frac{1}{2}$ garlic clove, minced
2 tablespoons lemon juice
I teaspoon chopped dill weed
2 teaspoons chopped capers
salt and freshly ground black pepper

I Beat the oil with the vinegar in a small bowl. Mash the hard-boiled egg yolks until smooth, then gradually add the oil mixture, beating well until blended.
2 Gradually add the mustard, garlic, and lemon juice, and mix well to form a creamy dressing. Fold in the dill weed, capers, and salt and pepper to taste. Serve lightly chilled.

Makes about I cup
Preparation time: 15 minutes

SPICY PEANUT DRESSING

Make this rich, spicy dressing in advance to allow the flavors to develop before using. It is the perfect dressing for the Indonesian vegetable salad Gado Gado, but is also delicious with grilled chicken, fish, or shellfish.

2 tablespoons creamed coconut
4 tablespoons milk
¹/₂ small onion, chopped
I garlic clove, minced
4 tablespoons smooth peanut butter
I teaspoon soft brown sugar
2 teaspoons soy sauce
¹/₂ teaspoon ground cumin
¹/₂ teaspoon chili powder
salt and freshly ground black pepper

I Chop the creamed coconut and place in a small pan with the milk. Heat gently for about 2 minutes, stirring constantly until the coconut melts and forms a paste with the milk.
2 Transfer the coconut mixture to a blender or food processor and add all the remaining ingredients. Process until smooth, then transfer into a small bowl. Cover and set aside until required.

Makes about ²/₃ cup
Preparation time: 10 minutes
Cooking time: 2 minutes

SHERRIED DRESSING

This rich, creamy, and distinctive dressing is perfect to serve with any fruit-based salad or a plain leafy salad assortment that includes Belgian endive or red chicory.

I egg
2 tablespoons dry sherry
2 tablespoons sugar
I tablespoon melted butter
juice of I orange
2 tablespoons lemon juice
4 tablespoons heavy cream
salt and freshly ground black pepper
chopped parsley, for sprinkling (optional)

I Beat the egg with the sherry, sugar, melted butter, orange juice, lemon juice, and salt and pepper to taste.
2 Pour this mixture into a small saucepan and cook over a low heat, beating constantly, until the mixture thickens. Do not bring to the boil. Set aside and allow to cool completely.
3 Beat the cream until it stands in soft peaks and fold it into the cooled dressing. Spoon into a serving bowl and sprinkle with the chopped parsley, if using.

Makes I cup
Preparation time: 15 minutes
Cooking time: 4–5 minutes

WARM CHICKEN, TARRAGON, AND ORANGE SALAD

1 x 3-pound chicken
1 medium onion, thinly sliced
grated zest and juice of 1 orange
1 tablespoon chopped fresh tarragon
(or ½ tablespoon dried)
1 bay leaf
1¼ cups water
1 tablespoon olive oil
½–1 tablespoon white wine vinegar
salt and freshly ground black pepper

Garnish:
1 small orange, thinly sliced
small bunch of watercress
tarragon sprigs (optional)

1 Put the chicken, sliced onion, orange zest and juice, tarragon and bay leaf in a large saucepan. Pour enough water over the top of the chicken to cover it and sprinkle with salt and pepper to taste. Cover, bring to a boil, and simmer for 45–60 minutes, until the chicken is cooked.

2 Lift the chicken out of the saucepan and leave to cool. Discard the bay leaf and onion. Measure the stock. Boil the chicken stock until it reduces to 1¼ cups. Set aside to cool, then chill in the refrigerator.

3 When the chicken is cold, take the meat off the bones, discarding the skin. Cut the meat into bite-sized pieces and place in a bowl.

4 When the stock has chilled, remove the layer of fat from the top, then reheat gently to thin it. Stir in the oil, and add wine vinegar, and salt and pepper to taste. Pour this dressing over the chicken and toss well.

5 Serve immediately, garnished with orange slices, watercress and tarragon sprigs if liked, or cover and chill until required. The salad may also be served on a bed of lettuce.

Serves: 4
Preparation time: 20 minutes
Cooking time: 45 minutes-1 hour

FRESH TOMATO DRESSING

Serve this dressing with a colorful mixed kidney and garbanzo bean salad. Canned tomatoes may be used
to make the dressing if plump ripe tomatoes are not available.

½ pound ripe tomatoes
2 tablespoons olive oil
I garlic clove, minced
I teaspoon paprika
salt and freshly ground black pepper

1 Place the tomatoes in a bowl and cover with boiling water. Let stand for 1 minute, then drain, and remove the skins. Halve and seed the tomatoes, then finely chop the flesh. Place in a bowl with the oil, garlic, paprika, and salt and pepper to taste, blending well.
2 Cover and chill until ready to serve. Toss well with the salad before serving.

Makes about ½ cup
Preparation time: 15 minutes, plus chilling

TOMATO VINAIGRETTE

6 tablespoons tomato juice
4 tablespoons extra virgin olive oil
2 tablespoons red wine vinegar
½ garlic clove, minced
¼ teaspoon sugar
I tablespoon finely shredded basil
salt and freshly ground black pepper

Beat together all the ingredients with salt and pepper to taste until well blended. Alternatively, place all the ingredients in a screw-top jar and shake vigorously to combine well before using.

Makes about I cup
Preparation time: 5 minutes

TOMATO, GARLIC, AND SUMMER HERB DRESSING

Try this dressing with pasta, rice, and grain salads; with cheeses; or with grilled lamb, chicken, or fish. It also makes a tasty dressing for summer vegetable salads based on avocado, asparagus, or beans.

1 pound ripe tomatoes, skinned, seeded, and finely diced
2 garlic cloves, minced
2 tablespoons balsamic vinegar
4 tablespoons extra virgin olive oil
6 large basil leaves, finely shredded
3 tablespoons chopped mixed fresh herbs, e.g. oregano, dill, chervil, chives, parsley, and mint
salt and freshly ground black pepper

1 Place the tomatoes in a bowl with the garlic, balsamic vinegar, and olive oil. Stir well.
2 Add the shredded basil and mixed herbs to the tomato mixture. Stir in salt and pepper to taste. Mix thoroughly to combine well. Let stand for at least 30 minutes before using to allow the flavors to develop and mingle.

Makes 1 1/2 cups
Preparation time: 15 minutes, plus standing

TOMATO AND PINE NUT DRESSING

Grilled asparagus sprinkled with slivers of Parmesan cheese is a perfect dish for this dressing. Serve as an appetizer with plenty of warm bread to mop up any extra dressing.

2 tablespoons balsamic vinegar
1-2 garlic cloves, minced
3/4 pound tomatoes, skinned, seeded, and chopped
5 tablespoons olive oil
1/2 cup pine nuts, toasted
sea salt flakes and freshly ground black pepper

1 Put the vinegar, garlic, chopped tomatoes and 5 tablespoons of the olive oil in a small bowl. Lightly season with the salt and pepper and mix well to combine. Alternatively, place the ingredients in a screw-top jar and shake vigorously to combine well before using.
2 Just before serving, add the toasted pine nuts to the dressing.

Makes about 1 cup
Preparation time: 15 minutes

ANGLER FISH SALAD WITH CILANTRO AND MINT DRESSING

Anglerfish (or monkfish, as it is often known) is an excellent salad ingredient,
as it has firm flesh and a very good flavor.

1 pound anglerfish, skinned and filleted
1 x 14-ounce can pimentos
(sweet red peppers), drained
5 tablespoons olive oil
1 tablespoon coriander seeds, crushed
1 onion, sliced
2 garlic cloves, minced
3 tablespoons capers, rinsed and drained
pared rind of ½ lemon, cut into
thin matchstick strips
4 ounces mixed salad leaves, to serve

Cilantro and mint dressing:
few sprigs of cilantro, coarsely torn
few sprigs of mint, leaves stripped
from the stems and torn
1 tablespoon balsamic vinegar or
lemon juice
salt and pepper

1 Cut the anglerfish into thin slices and set aside.

2 Rinse the canned pimentos under cold running water, then drain well and pat dry with paper towels. Cut the pimentos into strips.

3 Heat the olive oil in a large skillet. Add the coriander seeds and cook over a moderate heat for a few seconds. Add the onion and cook for about 5 minutes, stirring frequently until softened, but not browned. Add the garlic and cook for 1 minute.

4 Increase the heat to moderately high. Add the anglerfish slices to the skillet and cook, stirring gently, for 3-4 minutes, or until the fish is firm and opaque.

5 Lower the heat and stir in the pimento strips, capers, and strips of lemon rind. Remove the skillet from the heat and let cool for a few minutes. Remove the fish and set aside to cool. You can serve the fish warm or cold.

6 Make the dressing. Add the cilantro and mint to the liquid in the skillet. Stir in the balsamic vinegar or lemon juice. Season to taste with salt and pepper and toss lightly.

7 Arrange the fish on a bed of salad leaves on a serving platter, or on individual plates. Spoon the dressing over the top and serve.

Serves: 4
Preparation time: 15 minutes
Cooking time: 10 minutes

SWEET AND SOUR DRESSING

Plums give this dressing a fresh, tangy flavor. Try it with a ham salad or a simple salad of mixed leaves tossed with hot grilled bacon.

1 green onion
2 fresh ripe plums, pitted and finely diced
5 tablespoons olive or peanut oil
2 tablespoons sherry vinegar
2 teaspoons soy sauce
2 teaspoons tomato paste
1/2 garlic clove, minced
1/4 teaspoon soft brown sugar
salt and pepper

1 Cut the green onion into fine shreds, about 1 inch long. Place in a small bowl and add the diced plums. Add the remaining ingredients to the bowl and beat together until well blended. Alternatively, place all the ingredients in a screw-top jar and shake vigorously to combine well before using.

Makes 1 cup
Preparation time: 10 minutes

BELL PEPPER DRESSING

A Stilton and celeriac salad would taste and look wonderful with the vibrant tone of the red bell peppers.

2 red or green bell peppers
1 garlic clove, minced
1 teaspoon paprika
1/2 teaspoon mustard powder
4 teaspoons red wine vinegar
1/2 cup light olive oil
salt and pepper

1 Cook the bell peppers under a preheated hot broiler for 15 minutes, turning occasionally, until the skin is blistered and blackened all over. Alternatively, grill over hot coals. Transfer to a bowl, cover with paper towels and set aside.
2 When cool enough to handle, rub off and discard the charred skins. Cut each bell pepper in half and remove the seeds. Chop the flesh coarsely.
3 Place the grilled bell pepper flesh in a blender or food processor. Add the garlic, paprika, mustard, and vinegar, with salt and pepper to taste. Process until fairly smooth.
4 With the motor running slowly, carefully pour in the oil until the dressing is smooth. Adjust the seasoning to taste. Serve the dressing separately in a small jug.

Makes 1 1/4 cups
Preparation time: 5 minutes
Cooking time: 15 minutes

BLUEBERRY DRESSING

Spoon this dressing over a colorful mixed fruit salad of wild strawberries or raspberries, blueberries, grapefruit, and cooked chayotes.

½ cup olive oil
5 tablespoons blueberry vinegar
2 tablespoons minced red onion
1 teaspoon honey
salt and freshly ground black pepper

Beat the oil with the blueberry vinegar, onion, honey and salt and pepper to taste until well blended. Alternatively, place all the ingredients in a screw-top jar and shake vigorously to combine well before using. Shake the dressing once again before serving.

Makes about 1 cup
Preparation time: 5 minutes

THAI CHICKEN AND PAPAYA SALAD AND SPICY CHILI DRESSING

Papaya is often cooked or served with poultry or meat in Thailand as a cooling contrast to the spicy dressing. If papayas are difficult to obtain, mango, pineapple, or melon can be substituted.

Dressing:
2 small fresh green or red chilies, cored, seeded, and chopped
2 large garlic cloves, chopped
finely grated zest of 1 lime
juice of 3 limes
2–3 tablespoons nam pla (fish sauce)
2–3 teaspoons brown sugar, to taste

2 ripe papayas
1 crisp head lettuce, e.g. iceberg, with the leaves separated
½ large cucumber, thinly sliced
3 ounces bean sprouts
1 pound skinned chicken breast fillets
corn or peanut oil, for brushing

1 First make the dressing. Put the chilies, garlic, and lime zest in a mortar and pound with a pestle until crushed to a paste.
2 Stir in the lime juice and nam pla (fish sauce) until evenly mixed with the chili and garlic paste, then add some brown sugar to taste. Cover and set aside while preparing the salad ingredients and cooking the chicken.
3 Peel the papayas, cut each in half lengthwise, and scoop out and discard the seeds. Slice the flesh thinly.
4 Arrange the lettuce leaves around the edge of a serving dish, then place the papaya, cucumber, and bean sprouts attractively on top.
5 Brush the chicken breasts liberally with oil. Cook on the grill over hot coals for about 7 minutes each side, or until cooked to your liking. Alternatively, cook the chicken under a preheated hot broiler for about the same time.
6 Remove the chicken from the grill or broiler and place on a board. With a very sharp knife, cut it into bite-size diagonal slices. Arrange the chicken on top of the salad and sprinkle over the dressing. Let stand for a few minutes before serving.

Serves 4
Preparation time: 30 minutes
Cooking time: 15 minutes

YOGURT DRESSING

Sprouted alfalfa mixed with watercress, poppy or sunflower seeds and this creamy low-fat dressing
makes an unusual and healthy side salad.

²/₃ **cup plain yogurt**
I tablespoon lemon juice
I teaspoon clear honey
¹/₂ teaspoon mustard
salt and pepper

Beat the yogurt with the lemon juice, honey, mustard, and salt and
pepper to taste until smooth and creamy. Serve lightly chilled.

Makes ²/₃ cup

Preparation time: 5 minutes, plus chilling

VARIATION

For a mint yogurt dressing, mix ¼ cup plain yogurt with 3 tablespoons of mint jelly and
salt and pepper to taste, and blend well.

YOGURT AND BRAN DRESSING

Serve this substantial dressing with a cauliflower, bean and rice salad to add a splendid addition
to any buffet or vegetarian meal.

²/₃ **cup plain yogurt**
2 teaspoons natural bran
I tablespoon lemon juice
I small garlic clove, minced
dash of Tabasco sauce
I small onion, finely chopped
2 teaspoons chopped mint
salt and pepper

I Beat the yogurt with the bran, lemon juice, garlic, Tabasco sauce
to taste, half of the onion, half of the mint, and salt and pepper to
taste until well blended.
2 Spoon the dressing over the salad and sprinkle the remaining
onion and mint to garnish.

Makes about I cup

Preparation time: 15 minutes

PARSLEY AND GREEK YOGURT DRESSING

If served with a salad of Belgian endive (chicory), shavings of Parmesan cheese and croûtons,
you could use the leaves to scoop up the dressing.

5 tablespoons thick plain yogurt
I tablespoon chopped parsley
I garlic clove, minced
2 tablespoons finely grated Parmesan cheese
salt and pepper

I Put the yogurt in a small bowl. Add the parsley, garlic, and grated Parmesan. Stir in enough water to make a thin, pourable sauce and blend well to combine. Season with salt and pepper to taste and keep cool until ready to serve.

Makes ⅔ cup
Preparation time: 5 minutes

YOGURT AND HERB DRESSING

Pour this dressing over a summery salad of smoked chicken, chunks of pink grapefruit and orange,
sliced cucumber and lettuce leaves.

⅔ cup plain yogurt
I tablespoon lemon juice
I teaspoon clear honey
½ teaspoon Dijon mustard
4 tablespoons mixed chopped herbs, e.g. parsley, chives, tarragon, mint, or oregano
salt and freshly ground black pepper

Beat all the ingredients together with salt and pepper to taste in a small bowl until smooth and well blended.

Makes about ⅔ cup
Preparation time: 5 minutes

VARIATION

Low in fat and calories, you can vary the flavor of this dressing by adding chopped
herbs or gherkins, garlic, curry paste, or finely grated orange zest.

CRAB SALAD WITH LOW-CALORIE MAYONNAISE

I large cooked crab, about 2 pounds
1–2 tablespoons lemon juice
3–4 tablespoons low-calorie mayonnaise
(see below)
handful of fresh herb sprigs,
e.g. chervil, dill weed, parsley, cilantro
3 green onions, finely shredded
½ cucumber, peeled and finely diced
salt and freshly ground pepper
8 ounces arugula (rocket) leaves
lemon wedges, to garnish

Low-calorie mayonnaise:
2 hard-boiled egg yolks
I tablespoon white wine vinegar
I tablespoon lemon or lime juice
pinch of dried mustard powder
2 tablespoons low-fat plain yogurt
salt and pepper

I Remove the large claws and legs from the crab. Crack open with a rolling pin or small hammer and remove the white flesh. Flake into a bowl. Prise open the body of the crab. Remove any white meat and add to the bowl. Carefully remove all of the brown meat from the body and shell, discarding the inedible mouth parts, the grey stomach sac, and the feathery-looking gills. Add the brown meat to the bowl.

2 To make the low-calorie mayonnaise, mash the egg yolks with the vinegar, lemon or lime juice, mustard powder, and salt and pepper, to taste. Beat the yogurt into the egg mixture to blend well. Cover and let stand for 5–10 minutes to allow the flavors to develop. Any mayonnaise that you don't use can be kept, covered, in the refrigerator for 2–3 days.

3 Add the lemon juice and low-calorie mayonnaise to the crab, adjusting the quantities and seasoning with salt and pepper according to taste. Mix thoroughly.

4 Just before serving, arrange the rocket leaves on a serving platter or on individual plates. Scatter the herb sprigs over and pile the crab meat on to the platter or plates. Serve at once, with the green onion shreds, the diced cucumber and the lemon wedges.

Serves: 4
Preparation time: 30 minutes

LOW CALORIE VINAIGRETTE

Drizzle this light dressing over chilled leeks and capers. If you warm a lemon in a cool oven, it will produce more juice.

2 tablespoons lemon juice
3 tablespoons olive oil
I teaspoon Dijon mustard
I garlic clove, minced
I tablespoon chopped parsley
I tablespoon chopped chives
salt and freshly ground black pepper

Beat the lemon juice with the olive oil, mustard garlic, chopped herbs and salt and pepper to taste until well blended. Alternatively, place all the ingredients in a screw-top jar and shake vigorously to combine well before using.

Makes I cup
Preparation time: 5 minutes

LOW-CALORIE FRENCH DRESSING

Toss this slimming dressing with a crisp chopped apple, avocado, celery and pasta salad.

I tablespoon olive oil
6 tablespoons wine vinegar
$\frac{1}{2}$ teaspoon mustard
$\frac{1}{4}$ teaspoon sugar
salt and pepper

Place all the ingredients, with salt and pepper to taste, in a screw-top jar and shake vigorously until well blended.

Makes $\frac{1}{3}$ cup
Preparation time: 5 minutes

TOMATO JUICE DRESSING

Another low-calorie dressing—only 5 calories per tablespoon.

⅔ cup tomato juice
⅔ cup wine vinegar
I teaspoon grated onion
½ teaspoon dried mustard
I teaspoon sugar
½ teaspoon Worcestershire sauce
I teaspoon chopped parsley
salt and pepper

Beat the tomato juice with the vinegar, grated onion, mustard, sugar, Worcestershire sauce, parsley and salt and pepper to taste until well blended. Alternatively, place all the ingredients in a screw-top jar and shake vigorously to combine well before using.

Makes 1⅓ cups
Preparation time: 5 minutes

PINEAPPLE AND LEMON DRESSING

Serve with a fruit salad of bite-size cubes of pineapple and mango, sprinkled with plenty of raisins.

4 tablespoons lemon juice
or juice of I lemon
2 tablespoons clear honey
2 tablespoons unsweetened pineapple juice
I garlic clove, minced
salt and pepper

Beat the lemon juice with the honey, pineapple juice, garlic, and salt and pepper to taste until well blended. Alternatively, place all the ingredients in a screw-top jar and shake vigorously to combine well before using.

Makes about ⅓ cup
Preparation time: 5 minutes

LOBSTER SALAD WITH GREEN GODDESS DRESSING

2 pounds asparagus stalks
4 x 1-pound lobsters, freshly cooked
romaine lettuce leaves, for serving

Green goddess dressing:
1 small garlic clove, minced (optional)
3–4 anchovy fillets, well drained
1–2 tablespoons chopped chives
1–2 tablespoons chopped parsley
2 teaspoons chopped tarragon
1 cup low-calorie mayonnaise
(see page 58)
1 tablespoon tarragon vinegar
2–3 tablespoons sour cream (optional)
salt and freshly ground black pepper

1 Make the dressing. Put the garlic if using, anchovy fillets, and herbs in a food processor and process until well blended. Add the low-calorie mayonnaise and process to mix. Add the vinegar and salt and pepper to taste. Transfer to a bowl, cover, and refrigerate for at least 1 hour. Before serving, stir in a few tablespoons of sour cream, if wished.

2 Trim the woody ends from the asparagus stalks, making the stalks the same length. Then, if necessary, scrape the sides of each stalk with a swivel-bladed vegetable parer, starting about 2-inches from the tip. Cook the asparagus in a skillet of boiling salted water 4–8 minutes (depending on size), or until tender but still crisp. Drain and refresh under cold running water. Drain again on paper towels. Set aside to cool.

3 Crack the claws and tails of the lobsters and remove the meat. Keep the claw meat whole, and slice the tail meat across to form neat rounds.

4 Arrange the asparagus and lobster meat decoratively on a bed of lettuce leaves. Spoon over a little of the dressing and serve the rest separately in a small bowl.

Serves 4
Preparation time: 25 minutes, plus chilling
Cooking time: 4–8 minutes

INDEX